NOBODY CALLS ME DARLING ANYMORE

Nobody Calls Me Darling Anymore

Poems

Dannye Romine Powell

Press 53
Winston-Salem

Press 53, LLC
PO Box 30314
Winston-Salem, NC 27130

First Edition

Copyright © 2015 by Dannye Romine Powell

All rights reserved, including the right of reproduction in whole or in part in any form except in the case of brief quotations embodied in critical articles or reviews. For permission, contact author at editor@Press53.com, or at the address above.

Cover design by Kevin Morgan Watson

Cover art, "Two on a Table," Copyright © 2015
by Dawn D. Surratt, used by permission of the artist.

Author photo by Alyssa Romine

Printed on acid-free paper
ISBN 978-1-941209-24-0

For Lew, always

Acknowledgments

I am grateful to the editors of the following publications in which several of these poems (some in slightly different versions and with slightly different titles) first appeared.

32 Poems, "Anything Can Happen If the Ground Beneath Your Dwelling"
Bellevue Literary Review, "Because You Are Dead You Think You Can Have Anything You Want"
Birmingham Arts Journal, "Once There Was a Season"
Blackbird, "Confession," "Snow," "Tunnel of Green"
Cave Wall, "What the Child Saw"
The Charlotte Writers' Club Anthology, Volume 4, Journey Without, "Chamomile"
Connotation Press, "your nails your red red nails," and "Newlyweds"
Crab Creek Review, "Because She Does Not Know When She Will See Him Again, She Reads Obsessively about Fasting"
Crucible, "I Am the Girl"
Georgetown Review, "My Mother's Dead and Nobody Calls Me Darling Anymore"
Harvard Review Online, "Only Now Can I Admit"
Intimacy (anthology), "June Visit"
Iodine Poetry Journal, "Among the Things I Care to Keep," "The Story of My Birth," and "I Dream You Are Dating Maud Gonne"
Jelly Bucket, "This Was Our Lot and We Knew It," and "The Glance"
Kakalak, "The Sisters I Never Had"
Memoir (and), "Life without Us"
One, "Story"
Prairie Schooner, "On the Fifth Anniversary of My Mother's Death," and "My Mother Tells Me the Best Way to Dry Clothes"
San Pedro River Poetry Review, "He Washed Her Feet," and "It's Ritual Now," (as "One More Year")
Southern Poetry Review, "For Now"
storySouth, "The Night of the Big Wind in Ireland, 1839"
Tampa Review, "Love Poem, Almost," and "The Baby"
Tar River Poetry, "I Overhear My Husband Talking About Happiness"
Vin Master Anthology, "For Two Weeks After She Died"

"I Am the Girl" won the 2011 Randall Jarrell Poetry Prize, sponsored by the North Carolina Writers' Network.

"Because You Are Dead You Think You Can Have Anything You Want" was a finalist in the Bellevue Literary Review Literary Prizes, Fall 2014.

"Because She Does Not Know When She Will See Him Again, She Reads Obsessively about Fasting" was a finalist in the 2014 Crab Creek Review Poetry Contest.

"Story" was a finalist in the 2014 Atlanta Review Poetry Contest.

"The Night of the Big Wind in Ireland, 1839" was a finalist in the 2010 Hackney Literary Awards.

"Tunnel of Green" was a finalist in the 2012 Hackney Literary Awards.

"Once There Was a Season" won second place in the 2014 Hackney Literary Awards.

"Chamomile" was written during a winter residency at Yaddo in Saratoga Springs, New York.

Contents

I. THE BEARS COME HOME

Love Poem, Almost	3
your nails your red red nails	4
Your Face	5
Father	6
I Am the Girl	7
Recognition	8
Because She Does Not Know When She Will See Him Again, She Reads Obsessively about Fasting	9
Once in a Fevered Dream	10
After Her Stroke My Mother Tells Me The Best Way to Dry Clothes	11
The Dream of the Chinese Laundry	12
He Washed Her Feet	13
The Bears Come Home	14
Child Carrying Child	16
Confession	17
One Late Night in December	18
Among the Things I Care to Keep	19
Tunnel of Green	20
If The Ground beneath Your Dwelling	21

II. ONCE THERE WAS A SEASON

Hotel to Hotel	25
The Sisters I Never Had	26
June Visit	27
My Mother's Dead and Nobody Calls Me Darling Anymore	28
Newlyweds	29
The Baby	30
Lies	31
The Glance	32
What the Child Saw	33
The Story of My Birth	34
For a Couple of Weeks After She Died	35

Over the Line	36
Chamomile	37
I Dream You Are Dating Maud Gonne	38
The Night of the Big Wind in Ireland	39
Snow	41
Once There Was a Season	42
When the Other Shoe Has Dropped	43
This Was Our Lot and We Knew It	44
Dying, My Father Saw a Red-Haired Woman	45
Your Car Is Missing	46

III. THE VILLAGE OF YOU

After	49
The Old Hotel Is Empty	51
On the Fifth Anniversary of My Mother's Death	52
Only Today Can I Admit	53
Because You Are Dead You Think	54
In June, She Was All Angles	55
Neighbor	56
The Village of You	57
For Now	58
Is This What Hopkins Meant?	59
I Overhear My Husband Talking About Happiness	60
Stumbling onto a Description of Edward I's Corpse Found Preserved after 467 Years, I Realize How Badly I Want You to Last	61
Widow	62
It's Ritual	63
Life without Us	64
I Stand Staring at the Sky	65
Story	66
Author biography	71
Cover artist biography	73

I.

THE BEARS COME HOME

Love Poem, Almost

There I was, walking out
onto the porch, onto its long gray boards,
and I was thinking of you, of course,
and whether now that I lived in the country,
I would ever see you again. There were certain signs
that I had abandoned the world or it had abandoned me.
These were of no concern. My only intent was to walk out again
and again onto the porch, to marvel at how the gray boards stretched
into night. Believe me when I say I lived so deep
in the country that you would never, never have found me.

your nails your red red nails

always tapping my shoulder

say this   don't say that

this one   not that one

smile now   you will be happy

the way I wasn't
for none of the reasons you thought
were the right ones

you should see him now

the wrong one

Your Face

stained
and crumpled, outside

the glass window
of that massive oak door
and how night finally erased

everything else, steeples
and trees toppling
behind you, wind limping

away and how we stood fixed
in that tumult
of gazing, you on one side,
I on the other.

Father

You never said sorry,
never said good. Hated the way I ran,
the way I stood. Hated the way I peeled
an orange, thumb in the air
as I cut. *Learn to handle your mitts*, you said.
Learn. Learn. Winter. Summer. Turn. Turn
into a boy, is what you meant.

I Am the Girl

who waited at the high window,
spring breezes stirring
the room, and I
am the woman here now
in the silk dress
and ivory beads remembering
that girl whose breasts you describe
so clearly we can both see them
bared in the filtered sunlight
of these woods where we
have met to reminisce
about a time so distant that nothing
has faded, no one has come between,
and we are again that boy, that girl,
the breezes luscious as this peach we are sharing.

Recognition

That photo
in my mother's old album,

four people hiking
a rock-strewn path,
some shade, mostly sun,

but that one man,

that one, boot propped
on a stone—Who was he?
How did she know him?

I pointed. She turned away,
my beautiful mother,
and we were never the same.

Because She Does Not Know When She Will See Him Again, She Reads Obsessively about Fasting

beginning with Democritus
who lived forty days
by simply smelling honey
and hot bread
and on to the thousand Abyssinians
who traveled two months
to Cairo without provisions
subsisting on the sap
of acacia trees
and the Chelmsford woman
who for ten years survived
on a daily pint of tea, chewing
occasionally half a dozen raisins
or almonds but never swallowing
and finally the man from Bath
struck senseless
while walking in the woods
found at last and carried to Swan Inn
where he declared
he'd endured by sleeping
in the warmth of broad day
and dreaming of loaves and ale.

Once in a Fevered Dream

Once in a fevered dream
the wall beside my bed cracked
into crazy crooked lanes. I was young
and alone and didn't know the fever would break
and not break me.

A year or so later, in a foreign city, I fell
for a man who drove me mad
with what I thought was love. And maybe it was or,
if not, surely one of love's side roads veering off

through silvered birch. It was months
before that fever broke, months before my heart
reclaimed its perch. Then, one day, I heard the leaves
bandying his name, and the trees were whole and unhurt.

After Her Stroke, My Mother Tells Me the Best Way to Dry Clothes

Hang them, she says, in a roofless,
whitewashed structure
with wide-flung windows
on a mountainside in Italy.
How she carries on (though
she is from a small town in Georgia
and has never ventured abroad)
about the wide, glassy sea,
the air streaming uphill to caress
the garments inside,
the giant bed sheets dry
in a flash and the Damask
banquet cloths ready for the iron
in an hour. So vivid are her details,
that after she dies, I can't remember
if she'd imagined these airy structures
or I'd seen them with my own eyes,
which was always the way with my mother and me—
she'd dream the contours of a world
and I'd inhabit the village, hauling my laundry
up the mountainside, salt-stippled air
streaming through me.

The Dream of the Chinese Laundry

Press and mend,
ten hours a day, six days
a week, that was my job.
I loved it. Press
and mend. Steam rose up
to perfume me (if you can call
old sweat perfume). Sun billowed
into the room. The owner said
I was the best presser
and mender she had ever known.
I don't remember pausing for lunch
or taking a break. The giant white apron
covered my bulges. Press and mend.
I was so happy I hummed. I stood
facing a plate-glass window
but rarely looked up. I stopped
nagging my husband, stopped checking
on my sons. Press and mend. I stopped
trying to make up with everyone.

He Washed Her Feet

as she stood
in her bathing suit
in his tub, his two sisters giggling
at the door while he rinsed
the sand from her legs
and toes. Strange,
being at his house
with his mother off at work—
and the tub so mysterious,
deeper and paler than her own,
her bare feet touching
where she supposed he'd sat
naked to bathe. Why did all this rinsing
feel like a wedding or maybe
the way she'd imagined sex?
Wild and also sacred. She watched
the last of the grainy water glide
down the drain and rested her hand
on his shoulder as he toweled up
and down her legs. They were fourteen.
This was a long time ago.

The Bears Come Home

No way you could've known
they were heading your way,
staggering through
the woods to the house
you believed was yours because
you said it was
when anybody asked.
It felt like yours. It smelled
like yours. Father
in his club chair, reading
The Wall Street Journal, his beloved
Lucky lolling nearby. Mother
whipping eggs into froth
or slicing lattice for a cherry pie.
And you in your own small rocker,
reading aloud to your dolls. The three
of you the envy of all. No wonder
you ignored the scuffling outside
on the mat, the door flying open
as if with a great gust.

And now in they troop, reeking of wild
berries and roots. The silly old story
doesn't mention the yelling,
the dishevelment, how the bears
demolish the pie, wrestle
Father to the floor where he
lies in a stupor. It doesn't say
Mother's face collapses
into ruin or how
the golden-haired girl tears
up the stairs, flies out
the window for the high

limb of the oak, counting
backwards by fives, backwards
by tens. The old tale refuses
to warn us. It doesn't even hint.

Child Carrying Child

A new study suggests that a substance in the fluid surrounding a woman's egg beckons waiting sperm to swim over when the egg is ready to be fertilized.
—The New York Times, April 2, 1991

I sweep
the floorboards
in the attic, fill
a plastic bag
with grit. Everywhere
I turn, she's here
under the eaves. This child
now carrying her own child.
Her floppy pink doll my mother
named Rose, her books,
her baby clothes,
the faded dollhouse
I keep meaning
to give to Goodwill.

I wanted her to have it all—
take her easel
to the South of France,
dance the old dances,
the waltz, the tango. Finish
college. Live alone
in her own apartment, listening
to Mozart, growing
purple bougainvillea
on her wide white window sills.

In the evening, I crack
three eggs, watch the yolks float
in the clear glass bowl,
those slinky, come-hither globes.

Confession

I wash and wash
your little blue blanket
while my mother rocks you

and you grow hungry
while I wash the blue
blanket and my mother

warms the bottle
and feeds you while I wash
the little blue blanket,

pouring the Ivory liquid
into the warm water
and watching it flow

and dissolve, my hands, too,
dissolving in the water,
and you grow sleepy

while my mother holds you
and when you wake
she rocks you

and when you scream
she holds you
while I wash and wash

the blue blanket because
the little blue blanket
doesn't ever seem to come clean.

One Late Night in December I Search for the Green Velvet Box

and the earrings inside.
I want the box back, that old magic kingdom

that holds the gold,
you admiring their slow glimmer

and sway as I turn my face this way and that.

I waste the night
searching, sleep aching for that lost world

in my palm, how it sprang open

and closed.

Among the Things I Care to Keep

is the sight of my blond son
at two, his dad
lofting him high
to see Santa
hovering
in an air-shattering helicopter,
the child's heart
ricocheting
beneath his plaid jacket,
the three of us
shivering
in the strip mall's windy parking lot,
holding onto each other, holding on.

Tunnel of Green

sinking into deeper green,
gulls flapping
like circus tents.
I am walking,
walking, always
toward you, trapped
beneath a soft mat
of sky. There was a path
and I was on it.
Flat grass on either side.
Banyan trees. Wild birds, the likes
of which I promise you will never see.

———•———

So much has been lost
or ruined. Coral rock wall,
sweep of evergreen, orchids abiding
in trees. *Yes, orchids.* None of it ours,
none of it actual. Yet I lived there
for years beside you, breathing
in the sea, moving room
to room. That huge cage
of birds beneath the live oaks,
neighbors calling
to complain. I wish
I had asked one: Do you see me
at the window? Am I real?
Whose dust is this I sweep?

Anything Can Happen If the Ground Beneath Your Dwelling Was Once a Pleasure Park

A lake, boat house, flower gardens,
winding paths, gone long before
your time, the water drained
decades ago. Still, imagine!
A pavilion, a carousel,
a skating rink. In winter, you can see
the oval rim of the old lake,
its tricky depths now scattered
with leaves, a good-for-nothing creek
stitching its length. But on summer nights,
windows raised, you hear the whisper
of oars. And, once in awhile,
the scent of roses inviting you out,
and there you are, on a late July afternoon,
parasol in hand, swept to the edge,
a boat in the distance, a man
you once loved rowing toward shore.

II.

ONCE THERE WAS A SEASON

Hotel to Hotel

no one dying or deeply troubled,
luggage without rollers,
hotel to hotel,

no one drunk so our lives hung loose
as caftans
while the mangos ripened
red and gold

no one deeply troubled—
not even the aunts, who gathered
in the evenings to play the piano
and primp,

no one drunk—not even the uncles,
who shuffled cards into the night
and yammered on
about redheads and blondes,

hotel to hotel, luggage without rollers,
packing up our tennis racquets,

no one dying, so I failed to ask
for recipes and other practical instructions,

closets emptied, windows flung wide
to the endless sea,
palm trees rustling
in the rain-damp air,

no one drunk or deeply troubled,
and the red hibiscus
opening every morning.

The Sisters I Never Had or Why I Resist Going into Analysis

Of course, one was more beautiful
than the others. I hated her.
We all hated her, except for our father,
who invented games in order to embrace her.
Last time she wrote, she said she'd dropped
a hot iron on her foot. Hard as I tried,
I couldn't imagine her pain.

The next sister floated, her slim back
always in retreat. I'd find her name
scrawled in a book, erase it,
sign my own. After our parents died,
she wanted nothing but their stash
of worn maps. I imagine her heading west
on a train, reaching for something
in the overhead rack, something frilled,
maybe, made mostly of silk.

The last one—the baby—didn't live
to be ten. She would sleep
with her face fast to my neck.
Mornings, before the others woke,
she'd beg for stories. I'd tell her
about the twin cottages
where we'd live on a white beach,
watching each other's kids. I knew better,
knew she was no more than a comma,
tentative, shy, never meant to reach
the end of anything. Her kind
of vacancy takes a lifetime to fill.

June Visit

Wild azaleas in bloom,
heat escaping the pine straw—
and as I am about to leave, car engine
already running—my father steps to my window,
leans in and dangles before me, fresh from his garden,
the most luscious strawberry I've ever seen. And he lingers
there, grinning, unable to say what I long to hear: *For
you, sweet girl.* Or, *Come again soon, my child.*
But his words hang there before my lips:
plump, ripe, glistening.

My Mother's Dead and
Nobody Calls Me Darling Anymore

To hear the word, clear as a morning brimming
with sea, I've taken to saying it myself.
No, thank you, darling, to the girl at the door

selling wrapping paper. And, *Goodbye,
darling,* to my husband's aunt who calls
tonight from Texas to report a break-in.

Those last weeks at the nursing home,
my mother's vacant stare vanished when I walked in—
Darling, I'm so happy you're here. Come,

let me look at you, darling—the word lighting
on my shoulder like my childhood parakeet,
a smooth green against my cheek,

the way he nibbled at my ear
and cold mornings nudged his beak
up under my hair, barely arching his wings

before the fluffed shudder of settling in,
lifting one weightless foot, now the other,
sending chills, darling, all along my arms.

Newlyweds

She's planting seeds,
bulbs, anything she can sink
into the ground,
though it's still August,
hot and muggy
in the South.
The neighbors, curious,
watching from darkened windows,
agree she seems to prefer
gardening by moonlight,
on her knees,
allowing the cool soil
to drift
through her fingers.
They swear they've seen her
breeze into the house
for water, slam back out
for air.

The Baby

I take the baby—he's blond,
two months old—to a party. Music,
candles, scalloped ocean
out the patio door.
I put him on a table
with the other babies.
My baby wears a blue bunting
and only now, as I tell you this,
does it occur to me
that I do not even remove
the bunting.
What I do remove is myself.

When I remember him again,
he is gone. An empty table.

The party turns
into a search party.
Ambulances, helicopters,
an elongated net.

They fish him up,
hand him over.
This time, I fasten him to me,
lick his face,
lick his neck,
unzip his soggy bunting.

He is warm,
he is bawling,
my own lost baby,
salty as the sea.

Lies

Let's get to the bottom of this.
The whole matter

of disturbance,
for instance. Clatter

of roses opening
when it was over. Whack

of the missing tail
that will echo for years
though the cat has long since

basked
in its own completeness.

The Glance

A friend once told me
that nothing eventful
would ever again happen
in her life. You should've seen us
that day, outside on her steps,
sun fooling around
with our legs. Since,
she has married twice
and is now a Buddhist monk.
I hadn't a clue
about eventful back then,
not until that winter afternoon
I watched you fold your hand
into the pocket of your navy coat
and caught the glance
that flooded the back pastures of my heart.

What the Child Saw

The two of them
across the room pressed against

the window sill and her father's cigarette
as he watched her mother, his head tilted

back, eyes almost slits and her mother
in her brown silk dress, hip slightly thrust,

watching him in that way that was not exactly
sly but something else, yes, she can still see him

exhaling slowly, secretly, the smoke stroking
her mother's throat, her cheeks, the sky

behind them no longer blue but fuchsia now
and another color, one she's never been able to name,

and those clouds of smoke, floating, encircling,
the only thing that ever dared to come between them.

The Story of My Birth

Sly moon and chill. Her labor pains
have set in and still he insists they can't leave
the track—he's bet the daily double.
She pleads. He won't budge.

I knew none of this
until my father was dead. Strange
how my mother never laid blame
for what she said was a dry and difficult birth.
The nurses were changing shifts,
she'd say. *Confusion everywhere.*

From time to time, she'd remind me
how glad she was that night
for her new spring coat.
I just wrapped it around me,
and no one could tell my water had broken.

If my parents were alive to read this,
would they even recognize themselves?
Where does she get these wild tales? they'd say.

Believe me, I'd give anything
to erase those escapades—how
he'd cut across three lanes
of traffic to hang a quick left, how he'd race
to beat the bridge before it opened
over the bay, our lives almost catching on the edge.

For a Couple of Weeks after She Dies

my mother rides around
in the car with me. It's nice.
I like it. She doesn't ask if we are
running out of gas or if we are on the right
street. She doesn't say slow down, you're going to kill
all those cyclists over there or ask if something is wrong
with her door, she feels like she is about to fall out.
None of that. She sits upright, hands in lap,
and a new warmth spreads through me
as we drive through the autumn
sunshine. I can hear her,
but not really.

Over the Line

One summer night,
traveling late
along black curls
of road, my father,
too tired, to make it
into South Dakota—but hell-bent
on adding another state
to our list—parks
the green Chevy somewhere
along the even hem of North Dakota
and tells my mother and me
to stand in the middle
of the road and put one foot
over the line
into South Dakota.
So we balance there,
my mother and I—not daring
a single glance at each other—
as a warm prairie breeze swarms
our bare arms
and we plant our feet
across that invisible line
in what we will hereafter call
the wide dark of nowhere.

Chamomile

I hadn't thought of your old bachelor apartment
in years, the one where you stacked *Time*
on the pantry shelves and owned only one armchair—

deep-cushioned red leather. But this morning,
far from you and from home, I pour hot water
over my tea bag and the place floats back,

the framed photo of you smiling your Dylan smile,
the blue mountain bike an old girlfriend left behind
and how you'd rub my feet where my boots had pinched.

I loved you first for your uncluttered rooms
and spacious mind. No, not true. I breathe in this chamomile
and know I loved you for the taste of your lips
as you cradled me in the wild meadow of that red chair.

I Dream You Are Dating Maud Gonne

Not a pretty sight
you and the daunting Maud
in red dress and silver belt,
the two of you waltzing
in Chicago, slathered in lust.
It can't last, I console myself.
By now, she must be dry
as potato skins, while you,
my love, are a plump, ripe fig,
if slightly bruised and finely pecked.

The Night of the Big Wind in Ireland, 1839

All along Ireland's western seaboard people made peace
with their God, as I try to do now after my son calls again
drunk, this time to say he's taking off for the woods,

that I should come gather whatever I want
from his narrow loft with its wide bed and ragged
rubber tree. I sit frozen in my chair and continue reading

about Ireland's Big Wind, when, on the evening
of Saturday, January 5th, 1839, snow fell dense and heavy,
and by morning, a sky loaded with motionless clouds.

That afternoon, a stillness so profound
they say voices floated between farmhouses
more than a mile apart. I like to imagine my voice

floating to my son when he wakes from this binge.
Are you still alive? I whisper to air, and hear him reply:
I can't go on like this. Today's the day I stop.

But within hours, he's drunk again and hope melts
as fast as the snow on the 6th, when a band of warm air
shoved the cold east, followed at dusk by wind,

rains mixed with hail, more cold. Sometimes he's wretched
with regret, admits he's made a mess of his life,
though by now we've lost all trust, even when he's sober—

those short runs of fair weather, stars clicking
into place. I rarely heed the warnings that he's at it again:
edginess, that sketchy beard, a hoary film of worry

that descends. Then my dreams—he's falling off
a mountain or into a stream and lies broken somewhere
under branches. By midnight of the 6th, the wind spun

into gales and raged until dawn. Next morning, sun glazed
a wasteland, orchard walls down, slate roofs picked clean,
sea water streaming inland, flooding houses and shops,

gardens and barns, the smell of salt insinuating itself
for weeks. I know all about these smells, how they invade
every tributary of your being and render you senseless.

If my son won't stop this time, if he takes to the woods,
I'll do as I always do—climb his stairs, bucket and brush
in hand—and scrub as the Irish scrubbed, down on my knees.

Snow

on the daffodils.
You wore your blue hat
to re-fill the bird feeder. Hulls
on the white ground. In time, the missing
are often found, sometimes
not. I knew a woman whose son,
after years in an institution,
grew sane again. Hope expands
and contracts, like ice or hate.
When the birds returned this year,
I could see through to their hollow bones.
How I loathe their easy migrations,
their pesky hunger. You left your hat
on the hall table. The feeder is empty. Come home.

Once There Was a Season

when the clean branches
of winter trees
greeted me
like lit candles
and once
there was another season
when
the telephone
grew sweaty
in my palm
and my elbows
were always propped
on something hard
and the man
who answered
at the morgue
kept calling me lady
though I could tell
he didn't think I was
but he promised
over and over
to be in touch
if anyone
fitting your description
should happen to turn up

When the Other Shoe Has Dropped

A hush
not even the bees

can disturb.

Grass stops growing,
roses swallow their thirst.

At first, the naked eye
does not notice. Long exhale,

sharp intake.

Everything exactly the same,
only the wave has gone out
of the ocean.

This Was Our Lot and We Knew It

I tell you we trekked
for miles, women and children,

wore out our soles, encountered old lovers
grown slack in the gut. When we refused

their tired gambits, they fed us, hustled us
onward. The fish we carried

in baskets grew stiff. The hooks fell away
from their mouths. At dawn, we crossed bridges

on the outskirts of towns, glanced down
at grasses wild along streams.

We watched morning swim
the valleys, remembered how tempting

to mistake certain signs for peace,
though we said none of this aloud. Yes,

we wearied, but we kept moving. More towns,
distant mountains, a startling array of skies.

Dying, My Father Saw a Red-Haired Woman

on a bar stool
at the foot of his bed.

I wish she would leave,
he told my mother,

*so I could watch her
walk back in again.*

Your Car Is Missing and It's Only a Dream

But the anguish,
the disbelief.
It was right there.
I parked it
right there.
You are pointing
to an empty space,
the imprint
of the tires
in the grass,
the blades already
springing back,
the way
your father's pillow
plumped to life
moments after
they carried him out,
all so recent
you can almost feel
the warm fender,
the engine
still pulsing
where the car
once was.

III.

THE VILLAGE OF YOU

After

1.

I waited for you in the yard
and to pass the time,
tried to take a photo
of a cardinal. He sailed
from slate walk to garage
roof, back again. I steadied
my camera, imagined you
at the gate, watching,
wanting to surprise me.
The bird disappeared,
as did the sun. Dark flew in,
then cold. I kept aiming
the camera, hoping to hear you
whisper, *There, by the arbor.*
Hold still, and he's yours.

    2.

    I thought I'd find a letter from you,
one you might have mailed
on your way out
or handed to a stranger
with quick, specific instructions.
The familiar envelope, drifts
of white sheets, or maybe only one,
your fine, blue scrawl alive
on the page.

3.

You're at the kitchen window,
humble, willing to wait
out in the rain, always
in that soft blue shirt, the one
I loved. Is there something new
you want to say, something
never said? Last night,
you left a small, wooden box
on the back steps, gone, of course,
before I woke. I have set
a smooth round stone on the spot.

The Old Hotel Is Empty

and the ghosts float
through the blue evening,
floor to starry floor.

The louvered doors
once swung wide, balconies blinked
with lights. The ghosts go

in search of someone
to hold, to stroke. Their old wives?
Someone new and pink?

The night is corded
with gold and the girls outside
are shedding their clothes

to swim in the glassy sea.
The old hotel is empty and the ghosts
are alone in their loneliness

  drifting floor to starry floor.

On the Fifth Anniversary of My Mother's Death

That morning, chilly, the phone ringing so early
I suspected the news. Do I only imagine
you wore your blue gown
or were you wrapped in flannel?

This November morning, home from an errand
through trees never so golden,
I notice by the west wall the ginger lily,
one bloom tightly sealed, its fragrance deep
and hidden, like that last secret you held.
I'd press. You'd turn.

I still miss you, only now at odd moments.
In Paris last September, I ached
that you'd never drifted on the Seine
at sunset or drained the last of thick hot chocolate
at Angelina's, savoring the taste for blocks.

Not long ago, I found an old journal
where you'd made notes on Venice. I was a baby
when you were dreaming of those gondolas
floating above the ancient river.
Your words swam up my spine too late.

You died, leaving me
to keep piecing you together
like a worn map, where the roads
have been rubbed to oblivion.
Even today, your essence remains sealed,
its fragrance one I can neither catch nor hurry to unfurl.

Only Today Can I Admit

how much I hated wheeling my mother
into her room after lunch and hearing her say
this is not my room get me out
we are trespassing we will be arrested
and I would argue *look here is your bed*
with the pretty coverlet you picked out
last week and here the wing chairs
you had reupholstered before your stroke
and there the cranberry glass lamps
you found at the little shop on Coral Way
and everything you love is right here see
the photo of your granddaughter on the dresser
silly to think of anyone else with an identical
granddaughter and she would shake
her terrible white head *this is not my room*
this is not my room until I wanted to scream
and now these dozen years later I see that indeed
we were trespassing though I saw no signs
in the hall or on her door no signs anywhere
that said we'd strayed into the wrong hemisphere

Because You are Dead You Think You Can Have Anything You Want

You come back,
bent over my things
like a collector, hunched,
touching, wanting to lay claim
to everything. No, not everything.
Only what I cleaved to after you died.
My Moon Book, its midnight cover
and parchment pages, its luminous drawings
steeped in liquid gold. *Take the Limoges,*
I say, *The cut glass pitcher.* Please,
not the Moon Book, its cloth corners
worn, its ghostly pages drenched
with longing. *My Moon Book?*
I repeat, hoping I'd heard wrong.
Yes, you say, your hand outstretched.

In June She Was All Angles

auburn hair rippling
over one thin shoulder.
Yes, I remember
those days, a hundred
proms ago, a million
yards of tulle ago. Now
it's deep winter and she dozes
in her new roundness
on the white sofa
across from where I work
a thousand-piece jigsaw puzzle,
no rhyme or reason to it.
But patterns, always: These lines
horizontal, these waves
vertical, and here,
one long fish, maybe
an eel, gliding beneath
a ship heading east
or west, it's hard to tell,
and the almost-child
spinning, spinning in the deep.

The Village of You

Mind gone to cotton after the call
from the hospital early this morning,
and as we drive into the slow blades
of the hours, you say, *It won't be long now.*
We're making good time. Your voice

so deep an entire village springs up:
green-shuttered cottages at the edge
of the woods, a grocery
brimming with bread and cheese,
down the road a stone church
by a red-brick school, kids streaming
onto the playground, running
for see-saws, grabbing for swings
and me on a bench, under trees.

We haven't a clue what to expect.
The doctor had said hurry, and we do
and when we arrive, we find him alive
after all, which is not the point.
The point is how the teacher, the minister,
the grocer of you, allowed me to enter
the village of you and, for a time, reside.

For Now

spring has not breathed
its last, daphne still lingers in the hedge.
The baker inhales the grace
of his rising bread,
while his wife sets the table,
admiring her French clock on the mantel.
Of course there will be a knock at the door.
Isn't the messenger always threading
the woods, lace-up boots snapping
the twigs. *Rap-rap*, he practices
under his breath. *Rap-rap*.
For now, the baker bows his head, prays
the prayer he daily prays for his son,
who has finally begun to make his way
in the world. For now, the sky holds
and the butter glides golden onto the bread,
which, this moment, is fragrant and still unbroken.

Neighbor

His old hackberry
throws a blanket of shade
across our morning lawn. Our neighbor,
adding on, says the tree must go.
Its absence, I fear, will flood the yard
with too much light. What we've loved most
back here is the pebbled path
between garage and house. Soon,
that spot, too, will be so bright
we'll lose the loamy beds
of painted ferns and the border
of white impatiens. It was Larkin who said
sun destroys the interest
of what's happening in the shade.
The shade around the camellias
is where we hid blue marbles
for the child to find. And last week I sat here
on the stone bench re-reading
the letter that made me weep.
Neighbor, we will miss our shade.

Is This What Hopkins Meant

when he said,
Beauty is almost always gone?
That perfection lies
in those billowy moments
when we say goodbye,
holding open the door
for friends, ushering them
down the steps
and out into the ravine
of night,
or when we close our hymnals
and bow heads
as the casket is rolled
out into rain or sometimes
into the bright ache of snow.

I Overhear My Husband on the Phone Talking about Happiness

My husband does not talk
about happiness. He talks about taxes
and dampness in the basement
and how low to turn the heat while we sleep.
Is he having an affair? Did he get trapped
into a survey? Maybe he'd like roast lamb
for supper or, better, baked ham
with potatoes and chives. If he has begun
to wonder if he is happy, then must I
begin to wonder if I am happy?
Are we happy together? Apart?
Does it matter how happy we are
if we sit down together in the evening
and eat baked ham with potatoes and chives?

Stumbling onto a Description of Edward I's Corpse Found Preserved after 467 Years, I Realize How Badly I Want You to Last

His royal body (exactly how I think of yours)
in a coffin of yellow stone, enclosed in two wrappers,
one of gold tissue, strongly waxed
and fresh. His purple mantle (which, of course,
you'd shun), lined with white, studded with pearls
and red and blue stones. Most important: his face
(whose could compare with your own profile's
elegant loft?) entirely preserved beneath
closely fitted fine silk cloth. The hands were intact
as well as his feet, the toes distinct. (Wonder if
his big toe, like yours, declared its independence
from the herd?) Edward's length (hence,
the nick name "Longshanks") same as yours—
six-feet-two. And the gilt coronet of fleur de lis?
It's always there, especially when you sleep.

Widow

How the widow waits for her son to visit
from Berkeley or Atlanta in hopes,
while he's home, he'll trim the ivy
around the front windows, and, oh, he trims it
all right, but he always leaves two or three
ragged edges, which, of course,
she never mentions because the raggedness
is nothing compared with the envy
she knows she will arouse
in the coming weeks when she says
to her friends, *Just look at those windows.*
I waited months for my son to come home
and see how uneven he leaves
the edges! And she knows no one pays attention
because the women are not seeing
the unevenness. They are only imagining
her son in the kitchen, as it used to be,
for all of them, before their boys married
and moved far away. They can picture him
at her wooden table about dusk,
elbows propped, reading the paper,
or watching her, mindlessly, as she sets out
two plates, folds the napkins. How the silence
between them is soft as cotton, perfectly edged.

It's Ritual

this swift river, these loaf-like stones
we dig out each summer, drop
into canvas bags and haul

two hundred miles home to edge
the flower beds. So once again,
this green glade of a morning,
we wind down the mountain

to Gold Hill Road, park the car
on the same steep slope and wade
into the river that runs all year
in our minds. No wonder we keep

returning: this borrowed paradise,
this wide, dappled Eden, sun skimming
our backs. What we dare not say,
we lug between us up the ragged path.

Life without Us

Two empty swings
in the sloping back meadow
of a mountain house—ropes so long
the trees they hang from seem to stretch
to sky. Wooden seats, side by side, twisting a bit
in the summer breeze, as if the children,
who, seconds before, might've been pumping high
toward blue, squealing with joy, suddenly abandoned
their game. We stare down into this stranger's yard
without an inkling as to why sadness
settles over us like a shawl.

I Stand Staring at the Sky

Plowed fields
of clouds, deep gray

and fleeing east. At home,
they are waiting for supper. Our

dreamy near-child, her own child
growing inside. My husband hungry

and out of sorts. Still, I linger—rapt
beneath this swift, immaculate clearing.

Story

We had gone back
to our old summer place
with the low green trees
and the rhododendron's spent blooms,
where I had wept before
but now, wandering
room to room, holding
this new sorrow like a hapless child,
I could not weep and could not
settle, though somewhere deep
and all day long
I felt the familiar welling,
the windows swollen
shut, the lake sluggish
with rain and end-of-summer heat.

By September, we rounded
the slow curves of the mountains
for home, and we said,
or thought we said, *Maybe
he'll pick himself right back up
this time,* adept as we've become
at the shenanigans of hope.
But the papers had piled up,
and the mail
and the house
smelled of dying ferns.

Thanksgiving again
and we take our places
at the oval table, passed down
to us through generations, grateful
for everyone here. Our sons sit
opposite each other, the one
who struggles against the wind,
the one who glides.
The old story, alive again
in the wick of the waning year.
Bowls steam from hand
to hand, yellow leaves fly
at the windows. The afternoon
yawns and disappears. Someone
lights the fire, another starts
the coffee. The pattern so familiar
we could follow it blind, follow it back
through a hundred peeling years
or more, people we knew
and didn't know, the lucky
and the troubled, pulling up
to this table, pushing
back, some empty, some filled.

A Note from the Author

I owe a deep debt of gratitude to those friends who have read and critiqued these poems with insight, wisdom and kindness: Judy Goldman, Karon Luddy and Peg Robarchek; and to the members of the Friday afternoon poetry group, meeting now into a fourth decade, who have lovingly read draft after draft of individual poems as well as the entire manuscript, offering guidance, advice, encouragement and warm, mixed-berry pies: Lucinda Grey, Patricia Hooper, Susan Ludvigson, Julie Suk and Dede Wilson; and to my husband, Lew Powell, who swears he knows nothing about poetry but more often than not zeroes in on the wrong word, the clumsy phrasing, and instinctively knows always to begin each critique with, "I'm no expert, but ..."

DANNYE ROMINE POWELL is the author of three previous collections, two of which have won the Brockman-Campbell Award for the best book of poetry published by a North Carolinian in the prior year. She's won fellowships in poetry from the NEA and the North Carolina Arts Council and has won a residency to the writer's colony Yaddo, where she slept one icy winter in the bedroom once occupied by Sylvia Plath. She has worked for many years at the *Charlotte Observer*, where she is once again writing about books and authors. She is also the author of a non-fiction book, *Parting the Curtains: Interviews with Southern Writers*. She lives in Charlotte, North Carolina, with her husband Lew Powell, also a long-time journalist.

Cover artist DAWN D. SURRATT studied art at the University of North Carolina at Greensboro as a recipient of the Spencer Love Scholarship in Fine Art. She has exhibited her work throughout the southeast and currently works as a freelance designer and artist. Her work has been published internationally in magazines, on book covers, and in print media. She lives on the beautiful Kerr Lake in northern North Carolina with her husband, one demanding cat and a crazy Pembroke Welsh Corgi.

www.ingramcontent.com/pod-product-compliance
Lightning Source LLC
LaVergne TN
LVHW041345080426
835512LV00006B/613